The Adventures of
Huckleberry
Finn

Mark Twain

The Adventures of
Huckleberry Finn

Mark Twain

Abridged and adapted by Janice Greene

Illustrated by James McConnell

A PACEMAKER CLASSIC

Fearon Education
Belmont, California

Simon & Schuster Supplementary Education Group

Other Pacemaker Classics

The Adventures of Tom Sawyer
Crime and Punishment
The Deerslayer
Dr. Jekyll and Mr. Hyde
Frankenstein
Great Expectations
Jane Eyre
The Jungle Book
The Last of the Mohicans
Moby Dick
The Moonstone
Robinson Crusoe
The Scarlet Letter
A Tale of Two Cities
The Three Musketeers
The Time Machine
Treasure Island
20,000 Leagues Under the Sea
Two Years Before the Mast

Library of Congress Catalog Card Number: 90-82224

ISBN 0–8224–9351–9

Printed in the United States of America

1. 9 8 7 6 5 4 3 2 1

Contents

ADVENTURES OF HUCKLEBERRY FINN

Scene: The Mississippi Valley
Time: Mid 1800s

NOTICE: Persons trying to find a motive in this story will be prosecuted; persons trying to find a moral in it will be driven out of town; persons trying to find a plot in it will be shot.

BY ORDER OF THE AUTHOR

1 Me, Tom, and the Robber Gang

You don't know about me unless you have read a book by the name of "The Adventures of Tom Sawyer." That book was made by Mr. Mark Twain, and he told the truth, mainly.

Now this is the way that book winds up. My friend Tom and me found the money that the robbers hid in the cave, and it made us rich. We got six thousand dollars apiece—all gold. Well, Judge Thatcher, he took it and put it out at interest. It brought us a dollar a day apiece all the year round—more than a body could tell what to do with. Then the Widow Douglas, she took me for her son and said she'd civilize me. But it was rough living in a house all the time, seeing how awful regular and decent the widow was in her ways.

So when I couldn't stand it any longer, I lit out. I got into my old rags and my shed again. Then I was free and satisifed. But Tom Sawyer, he hunted me up and said he was going to start a band of robbers. He said I could join if I went back to the widow and was respectable. So I went back.

Well, the widow she cried over me and called me a poor lost lamb, and the whole thing started up again. She put me in them new clothes, which made me sweat. She rang a bell for dinner and you had to come on time. She wouldn't even let me smoke, though she took snuff herself.

That night after dinner, Miss Watson, the widow's skinny old sister, started pecking at me. She told me all about the bad place where some people go after they die. I said I wished I was there. She got mad then, but I didn't mean no harm. All I wanted was a change.

By and by they brought the slaves into the house and had prayers. Then everybody was off to bed. I went to my room with a piece of candle and set down in a chair by the window. I tried to think of something cheerful, but it wasn't no use. I felt so lonesome I most wished I was dead. Pretty soon a spider went crawling up on my shoulder. I flicked it off and it went right into the candle. I didn't need anybody to tell me that was an awful bad sign that would fetch me some bad luck.

I sat down, a-shaking all over, and got out my pipe for a smoke. Pretty soon I heard a "*me-yow!*" down below. I said, "*me-yow!*" soft as I could. Then I slipped out the window to the ground. Sure enough, there was Tom Sawyer waiting for me.

We went tiptoeing along a path toward the widow's garden when I fell over a root and made a big noise. Miss Watson's big slave, Jim, was there by the kitchen door. He says, "Who's there?" Jim tiptoed down the path and sat down and waited for the noise to come again. By and by he began to breathe heavy and to snore.

I was in a sweat to get away, but Tom had to play something on Jim. So he slipped Jim's hat off and hung it on a tree right over him. Afterward, Jim said that witches put him in a trance! He said they rode him all over the state and then set him under the trees again.

Tom and me met up with Jo Harper and Ben Rogers and some of the other boys. We borrowed a boat and went across the river to a cave Tom knew about. Then Tom laid out his plan for a robber gang. First we had to sign our names in blood. We took an oath that if anyone told the gang's secrets, his family would be killed by the rest of the gang. Ben Rogers says, "Here's Huck Finn, he ain't got no family. What you going to do about him?"

"Well, ain't he got a father?" says Tom Sawyer.

"Yes, he's got a father. But he ain't been seen in these parts for a year or more."

They talked it over and they was going to rule me out. I was most ready to cry when all at once I thought of Miss Watson—they could kill her. The boys said she would do. Then Tom told us how we was going to be high-toned robbers—just like in the books he'd read. We'd stop stages and kill people

and take their watches and money. It took us most of the night to settle everything. We elected Tom Sawyer first captain and Jo Harper second captain. I got back to the widow's house just before day was breaking. My new clothes was dirty and I was dog-tired.

In the morning I got a good going-over by Miss Watson on account of my clothes. But the widow, she didn't scold. She just cleaned them up. Then Miss Watson got me to pray. She told me that praying would get me whatever I asked for. But I couldn't make it work when I tried for some fishhooks. When I asked the widow about it, she said what a body got from praying was gifts to the spirit. She said it meant that I must help other people and never think about myself. I turned it over in my mind, but I couldn't see no advantage—except for other people.

About this time, they found a man drowned in the river. People was saying it was my Pap, but I had a feeling it wasn't him. Pap hadn't been seen for more than a year. I didn't want to see him no more. He used to always whale me when he was sober and he could get his hands on me. I used to take to the woods most of the time when he was around. I judged the old man would turn up again by and by, though I wished he wouldn't.

We played robber now and then about a month, and then I quit. All the boys did. We hadn't robbed nobody and hadn't killed any people. We'd only just pretended. We used to hop out of the woods and go charging down on hog-drivers and women in carts taking garden stuff to market. But we never did anything to them.

Well, three or four months run along, and it was well into winter now. I had been going to school and could spell and read and write just a little. The longer I went to school, the easier it got to be. I was sort of getting used to the widow's ways, too.

One morning I seen somebody's tracks nearby the house. I didn't notice anything at first, but next I did. There was a cross made with big nails in the left heel of the boot. Quick as I could, I went to Judge Thatcher's. I told him I wanted him to take my money—all of it. He says, "Why, what can you mean, my boy?"

"Please take it," says I, "and don't ask me nothing. Then I won't have to tell you no lies."

But he wouldn't take it. He gave me a dollar and I left. That night, when I lit my candle and went up to my room, there sat Pap!

2 Two Runaways

He was almost 50, and he looked it. His hair was long and tangled and greasy. As for his clothes—just rags, that was all. He kept a-looking at me all over. He says, "Very dressed up. Very. You think you're something, *don't* you?"

I says, "Maybe I do and maybe I don't."

"Don't you give me none of your lip," says he. "I hear you've been to school—can read and write. You think you're better than your father now, because he can't. *I'll* take it out of you. Just let me catch you fooling around that school again, you hear? I'll tan you good."

He sat there a-mumbling and a-growling a minute. Then he says, "I ain't been in town two days, and all I hear about is you being rich. You git me that money from Judge Thatcher tomorrow—I want it."

"I ain't got no money. You ask Judge Thatcher. He'll tell you the same."

"All right, I'll ask him. And I'll make him pay up, too."

But Pap couldn't get a cent out of Judge Thatcher. So every now and then I'd borrow two or three dollars off the judge for Pap to get drunk on. It kept him from beating me.

Pap got to hanging around the widow's too much. So she told him that if he didn't quit coming around she'd make trouble for him. He said he would show them who was Huck Finn's boss. So one day he catched me. He took me in a boat about three miles up the river. Soon we got to a log cabin hid there in the woods.

We fished and hunted, and our catch was what we lived on. The widow found out where I was, and she sent a man over to try and take me back. But Pap drove him off with his gun.

A couple of months went by and I got used to being where I was. I didn't see how I'd ever got to like it at the widow's. There, you had to go to bed and get up regular, and have old Miss Watson pecking at you.

But Pap got to beating me all the time. I couldn't stand it. He'd go away a lot, too, and lock me in. I made up my mind I was going to run off. One day when he was gone, I found an old rusty saw blade stuck up between the boards of the roof. I went to work on one of the logs in the corner under the table. It was a good long job, but I had a hole most sawed through by the time I heard Pap coming. I figured I could crawl through the hole that night if he got drunk enough.

After supper, Pap got the jug, and drank and drank. He tumbled down in his blankets by and by, but didn't go sound asleep. Before I knew it, I was asleep.

When I woke, Pap was on his feet, holding his knife and looking wild. He called me the Angel of Death, and said he would kill me. I begged, and I told him I was only Huck. But he laughed such a screechy laugh, and roared and cussed, and chased after me. Once he made a grab and got me by the jacket. I thought I was gone, but I slid out of the jacket quick as lightning and saved myself. By and by he wore out and dropped down with his back against the door. He said he would rest a while and then kill me. But he dozed off pretty soon.

Next morning Pap didn't know nothing about what he'd been doing. He sent me off to the river to see if there was a fish on the line for breakfast. I noticed some branches and such things floating on the water, so I knew the river had begun to rise. Back when I lived in town, the rise used to be great times for me. There's always cordwood and pieces of log rafts floating down, and all you have to do is catch them and sell them to the sawmill.

I went along the bank with one eye out for Pap and the other looking for anything the river might bring along. All at once, a canoe about 13 foot long comes floating down. I figured she must have broken loose as the river began to rise. I dove in and got hold of her. First I thinks the old man will be pleased. She's worth ten dollars. Then I had an idea. I figured I'd take her when I run off. So I hid her good. When I got back, Pap was angry with me for being so slow with the fish line. But I just told him I fell in the river.

Pap wanted to go into town, so about half-past three he locked me in and left. I waited till he had a good start. Then I got the saw and went to work on the log. Before Pap was across the river, I was out.

I took a sack of cornmeal and the bacon. I took all the coffee and sugar. I also took the frying pan and the coffee pot and the fish line and the matches. I took everything in the cabin that was worth a cent and loaded it into the canoe. Then I shoved the log back into place and covered up the sawdust. If you didn't know it was sawed, you wouldn't ever notice it.

I went off with the gun looking for birds, when I see a wild pig. I shot the pig and hauled him back to the cabin. I smashed in the door with the ax and brought in the pig and let the blood fall on the ground. Next I filled an old sack full of big rocks and dragged it to the river and dumped it in.

I figured they would follow the track of that sack of rocks to the water's edge and then drag the river for my body. They'd soon get tired of that and wouldn't bother no more about me.

I climbed into the canoe and paddled off toward Jackson's Island. I knew that island pretty well. Nobody ever came there. It seemed like a good place for me to live. I reached it just as the sky was turning gray. I pulled the canoe up to the bank and into some thick willow branches. Then I stepped into the woods to sleep.

The sun was so high when I woke up, I figured it must be eight o'clock. I was laying there feeling lazy and comfortable, when I hears a "boom." A ferryboat was coming along, firing its cannon. They always fire a cannon when someone's drowned, to make the body come up. The boat came near, and I see Pap and Judge Thatcher, Tom Sawyer and his guardian, Aunt Polly, and his brother Sid and plenty more. I knew I was all right now. Nobody would come looking after me.

Three lonesome days and nights went by. I fished and picked berries and explored around. Then, while I was chasing after a snake, I bounded right into the ashes of a campfire that was still smoking.

My heart jumped up. I went sneaking back as fast as I could. That night, I slept in the canoe, but I didn't sleep easy. By and by I says to myself, I'm a-going to find out who's on this island with me, or bust.

Just as day was coming, I found the campfire again. And there, sleeping on the ground, was Miss Watson's slave, Jim!

Well, Jim was sure I was a ghost. But pretty quick he knew I wasn't dead after all. I was ever so glad to see him. I weren't lonesome no more. I told him about how I got away from Pap. Then I says, "How do you come to be here, Jim?

Jim made me promise not to tell. Then he says, "I—I run off!"

"Jim!"

"But mind, you said you wouldn't tell. You know you said you wouldn't tell, Huck."

"Well, I did, and I'll stick to it. People will call me a low-down Abolitionist. But that don't make no difference. I ain't a-going to tell."

Jim tells me he run off when he learned Miss Watson was going to sell him down to New Orleans for 800 dollars. He figured he was rich now. He says, "I owns myself, and I's worth 800 dollars. I wish I had the money, though."

3 Danger on the River

The river went on rising and rising. One night we catched a raft that was 12 foot wide and about 15 foot long.

Another night here comes a two-story house floating along. We went out in the canoe and got aboard. There was heaps of old greasy cards scattered around over the floor, and whisky bottles. And there was something lying in the far corner that looked like a man. Jim went over to see. He said it was a dead man, shot in the back. He told me not to look, but I didn't want to see him anyway.

We got a lot of stuff: an old tin lantern, two dirty old calico dresses and a sunbonnet, a fish line, a lot of candles, and plenty more.

When we got back to camp, I wanted to talk about the dead man and guess how he come to be killed. But Jim didn't want to. He said it would bring bad luck.

Well, a couple of days went by. I figured I would slip into town and see what was going on. So one night I got into one of the dresses and the sunbonnet, and I paddled up the river. At the end of town, I see a light in a house that hadn't been lived in for a long time. I peeped in the window and saw a stranger, a woman about 40 year, knitting.

I knocked on the door. She says come on in and take a chair. I says my name is Sarah Williams and I've walked all the way from Hookerville, seven mile, to see my uncle. She wanted me to stay the night, but I said I'd rest a while and go on. She got to talking about her family and about coming to live in this town, and by and by she got around to the murder.

She tells me they think Pap might have done it. Pap or a runaway slave—Jim!

She says: "The slave run off the very night Huck Finn was killed. There's a reward out for him—300 dollars. Some folks think the slave ain't far from here. I'm one of them, but I ain't talked it around. The other day I was pretty certain I'd seen smoke on that island over yonder they call Jackson's Island. My husband and another man are going over there after midnight tonight."

I got so uneasy I couldn't sit still. I had to do something with my hands. I took up a needle off the table and went to work threading it. The woman started looking at me pretty curious and smiling a little. She says, "Come now, what's your real name? Is it Bill, or Tom, or Bob?"

She looks at me very kind. She says she knows I'm a runaway apprentice, but she won't tell on me. So I

says I'd been bound out to a mean old farmer, and I've run away. She says she spotted me for a boy when I threaded that needle.

"Hold the needle still and poke the thread through it. That's how a woman does it. A man does it by holding the thread still and bringing the needle up to it. Now trot along, child. If you get into trouble you can send word to Mrs. Judith Loftus, which is me."

She let me go, and I was off in a hurry. Back at camp I woke up Jim and says, "Git up! They're after us!"

16

We loaded all we owned on that raft and on the canoe. Then we slipped down the river, never saying a word.

We traveled nights. When daylight came, we'd tie up the raft and cover it with branches and sleep a while. Jim took up some top boards on the raft and made a snug wigwam for us to sleep in.

A few nights below St. Louis, we had a pretty big storm. I spotted a steamboat that had killed herself on a rock. I wanted to land on her, but Jim was dead set against it. I says, "Would Tom Sawyer pass up an adventure such as this?" Jim grumbled, but he give in.

We climbed up on her and went sneaking down the deck, feeling our way in the dark with our feet. We came to the hallway where they had the officers' rooms and, by Jiminy, we see a light!

Jim whispered that he was going for the raft, and he left. But I couldn't rest till I seen what's going on. I heard a voice call out, "Oh, please don't, boys. I swear I won't ever tell!"

Another voice says, "That's a lie, Jim Turner. You've always gotten more than your share because you swore if you didn't, you'd tell. But now you've said it one time too many."

I crept along till I see a man tied hand and foot, and two men standing over him. One was holding a lantern and the other a pistol. The man with the lantern says, "Put away that pistol, Bill."

"I don't want to, Jake Packard. I'm for killing him."

Then Packard says to Bill, "Come on in here."

He walked in my direction. I crawled back into one of the rooms and into an upper bed as fast as I could. The two men come in, and stand so close to the bed I could have touched them.

Packard talked low. "Let's go through the rooms and gather up anything we've missed. Then we'll shove off and wait. I say it ain't a-going to be more than two hours before this wreck breaks up. See? Turner will be drowned, and won't nobody be blamed for it. I don't want to kill a man as long as you can git around it. It ain't good morals. Ain't I right?" Bill agreed, so off they went.

I lit out, in a cold sweat. I whispered, "Jim!" and he's right there, at my elbow.

I says, "Quick, Jim, there's a gang of murderers in there. If we don't hunt up their boat and set it loose, one of them's going to be in a bad fix. But if we find their boat we can put 'em *all* in a fix—for the sheriff will get 'em. Quick! You start for the raft—"

"Oh lord, the raft broke loose—and here we are!"

4 Protecting a Friend

Well, I catched my breath and most fainted. We had to find that boat now—had to have it for ourselves. So we went a-quaking around the deck and finally we spotted her. In another second we'd a-been aboard her, but just then a door opened. Packard flung something in the boat and got in. Then Bill got in after him.

I felt so weak I could hardly stand it. But Bill says, "Hold on—did you search him?"

"No," says Packard. "Didn't you?"

"No. So he's still got his share of the cash."

So they went back inside to get it from him. I tumbled into the boat and Jim after me. I got out my knife and cut the rope, and away we went!

We boomed along, looking for our raft. I got to thinking how awful it was, even for murderers, to be in such a fix. We found the raft by and by, and I told Jim I'd head for shore and try to find some help.

I paddled toward some lights on shore. As I come close, I seen a village. Nearby, there was a ferryboat. I found the watchman and woke him up. I started to cry and told him about how my pap and mam and sis were all on board that wreck, and so was Miss

Hooker. The watchman said he'd *like* to go out and rescue them, but who was going to pay for it? So I let on that Miss Hooker had an uncle who was rich, and that got him going quick enough.

I was waiting to see the ferryboat leave when along comes the wreck! A kind of cold shiver went over me. She was mostly sunk, and I see in a minute there weren't much chance of anybody being alive in her. I pulled all around her and hollered a little, but there wasn't any answer.

Next morning we looked over the stuff the gang had stole off the wreck. There was blankets and clothes, a lot of books and three boxes of cigars. The cigars was prime. I read Jim a lot from the books about kings and dukes and such. I told him about the Dauphin, the son of King Louis XVI of France. He was supposed to become king, but they shut him up in jail. Some say he escaped to this country.

We figured that three more nights would get us to Cairo, where the Ohio River comes in. Then we'd go up the Ohio, to the free states, and be out of trouble.

Well, the second night a fog come on. I set off in the canoe and tied the raft line to a little tree. But the raft came booming along so fast she tore the tree out by the roots—and away she went. I was so sick and scared I couldn't budge for a minute. Then there wasn't no raft in sight.

I shot out the canoe into a solid white fog, and had no idea where I was going. Away down somewhere I hear someone give a whoop, and my spirits rise. I went tearing after it. Next I hears a whoop in one direction, and then another, till I was tangled up good.

I got into a lot of little islands, and it got even worse trying to chase down the whoops. By and by I seemed to be in the open river and I couldn't hear a whoop nowheres. I figured maybe the raft had hit a snag and it was all over for Jim.

It was near daylight when I finally did find the raft. Jim was sitting with his head between his knees, asleep. The raft was littered with leaves and branches and dirt. So she'd had a rough time.

I got aboard and laid down. Then I stretch my fists out and says, "Hello, Jim, have I been asleep?"

Jim woke up and says, "Goodness gracious, is that you, Huck? You ain't drowned? It's too good for true, honey, it's too good for true."

I says, "What's the matter with you, Jim? You been a-drinking?"

I made out that nothing happened at all. By and by Jim figures he must have dreamed the whole thing. By now it was getting light and you could see all the branches and dirt pretty plain. I pointed them out and asked him what those stood for.

Jim looked at the trash and at me. Then he looked at me straight, without smiling and says, "What do they stand for? I'll tell you. When I was all wore out working the raft and calling for you, my heart was mostly broke because you was lost. And I didn't care no more what happen to me. And when I wake up, and find you safe, the tears come, I was so thankful. And all you was thinking was how you could fool old Jim with a lie. That stuff over there is *trash*, and trash is people that shames their friends."

He got up slow and went into the wigwam. It was 15 minutes before I could work myself up to go and humble myself to him. But I done it, and I wasn't ever sorry for it afterward, neither.

As we got closer to Cairo, Jim said he felt all trembly and feverish because he was so close to freedom. Well, *I* was all trembly and feverish because he was going to be free and I was to blame for it. My conscience got to stirring me more and more. At last I thinks, it ain't too late—I'll paddle ashore as soon as we see a light, and turn him in.

By and by a light showed, and I told Jim I'd go and see if that was Cairo. I shoved off in the canoe and Jim calls out: "Pretty soon I'll be a-shoutin' for joy, and it's all on account of Huck. You're the best friend Jim's ever had. And you're the *only* friend Jim ever had."

Well, I just felt sick, but I figures I got to tell. Right along comes a boat with two men in it with guns. They stopped and I stopped. One of them says, "You belong on that raft over there?"

"Yes, sir," I says.

"Any men on it?"

"Only one, sir."

"Well, there's five slaves run off tonight up yonder. Is your man black or white?"

I tried to answer right away, but I couldn't. Finally I says, "He's white."

He says, "We'll just go see for ourselves."

I said I wish they would because pap and mam and sis is there in the wigwam, sick. And everybody goes away when I try to get some help.

Well, they figured we all had smallpox, so they cleared out quick as they could. I went back feeling low, because I'd done wrong. Then I says to myself, suppose I'd done right and told on Jim? Would I feel any better? No, I'd feel just as bad. So I figured I wouldn't bother no more about it.

5 A Deadly Feud

The next night got gray and thick. It was very late when a steamboat comes up the river. We heard her pounding along, but we couldn't see her till she was close. Then all of a sudden she was right there, with her wide-open furnace door shining like red-hot teeth. People yelled at us, and the bells jingled for the engine to stop. Then as Jim and I dove overboard, she come smashing straight into the raft.

When I come up I didn't see Jim. I hollered about a dozen times, but didn't get any answer. So I grabbed onto a loose board and shoved along to the shore. There I see a big old-fashioned log house. Before I could walk past, a lot of dogs swarmed around me, barking and howling. I knew better than to move.

They called to me from the house. They said to come forward and walk slow. Inside three big men pointed their guns at me. I was plenty nervous. One of them asked if I knew some people named the Shepherdsons. I said I didn't, and they seemed satisfied. They said I didn't look like a Shepherdson, anyway.

Then they set down a heap of food for me to eat. I told them my family was all dead or gone away. I'd

been traveling up river on a steamboat when I fell overboard and swam ashore near their house. They said I could have a home here as long as I wanted it.

The family was called the Grangerfords, and they were mighty nice. Old Colonel Grangerford was a gentleman, and everybody loved to have him around. Bob was the oldest son and Tom next—tall men with broad shoulders and black eyes. Then there was Miss Charlotte, tall and proud and beautiful. Miss Sophia was beautiful, too, but gentle and sweet. Last was Buck, who was about my age, 13 or 14.

One day Buck and me was out hunting when we hears a horse coming. Buck says, "Quick, jump for the woods!"

We done it, and pretty soon a handsome young man come riding along. I knew it was Harney Shepherdson because I'd seen him at the steamboat landing. He sat straight as a soldier, with his gun across his saddle. I heard Buck's gun go off at my ear, and Harney's hat tumbled from his head. Harney grabbed his gun and rode straight to the place where we was hid. But we didn't wait. We started through the woods on a run. Harney fired a couple of shots, and then he turned around and rode back the way he come. We never stopped running till we got home.

Buck told me his family had a feud with the Shepherdsons. That meant the families were warring against each other, and it wouldn't end till everybody was killed off. Noboby could remember how the feud got started in the first place.

Next Sunday we all went to church. The Shepherdsons were there, too, and everybody had their guns handy. Afterward, when we'd had lunch and everybody was dozing around, Miss Sophia took me into her room. She told me she'd left her Testament at church. She wanted me to go get it for her and not say nothing to nobody. I went along and found it. Inside was a little piece of paper with "Half past two" written on it. I puzzled over it but couldn't make anything out of it. Miss Sophia was mighty glad to see it, and said I might go and play now.

I was going down to the river when Jack, the slave they give me, asked me if I wanted to see some water moccasins. I think that's mighty curious. Noboby wants to see water moccasins. So I says, all right.

He leads me through a swamp to a place that's all thick with trees—and there's Jim!

I figured he'd be surprised to see me, but he wasn't. He said he swum along behind me that night and heard me yell. But he didn't dare answer because someone might come pick him up. Then Jim told me the raft hadn't been all smashed up like I thought. He'd been patching it up, and now it was almost ready to go.

I don't want to talk much about the next day. I got up about dawn and the house was empty. I found

Jack, and he tells me Miss Sophia's run off with Harney Shepherdson! The women had gone to stay with relations. And the men took off to try to kill Harney before he got across the river with Miss Sophia.

I ran up the river road and by and by I begin to hear guns. I come in sight of the steamboat landing and the log store. Then I climbed up a tree that was a little in back of a woodpile, to see what was going on. Next to the store was another woodpile and two boys were hiding behind it. They was shooting at four or five men on horses. One of the boys takes aim and hits a man. The men jumped off their horses and dragged the hurt one toward the store.

Just then the boys started on the run. The men seen them and come after them, but the boys had too good a start. They got to the woodpile in front of my tree. The men tried a few shots at them, but no luck. So they rode off. One of the boys was Buck and the other was a chap about 19.

Buck was awful surprised to see me. He started to cry and told me his father and two brothers had been killed. He said he and his cousin Joe (that was the other chap) would make up for this day yet. I asked him what became of young Harney and Miss Sophia. He said they'd got across the river and was safe. I was glad of that. But Buck went on and on because he didn't manage to kill Harney that day. I ain't ever heard anything like it.

All of a sudden, bang! bang! bang! goes three or four guns. The men had slipped around through the woods and come in behind without their horses! The boys ran to the river and jumped in—both of them hurt. As they swum down the current, them men run along the banks shooting at them and calling out, "Kill them, kill them!" It made me sick. I ain't a-going to tell all that happened. I wish I hadn't ever come ashore that night to see such things.

I didn't come down from the tree till it begun to get dark. I pulled Buck and the other boy from where they were floating in the river, and covered up their faces. I cried a little when I covered up Buck's face. He'd been mighty good to me. Then I made straight away for the swamp. I never felt easy till Jim and me was out in the middle of the river, free and safe once more.

6 The King and the Duke

Two or three days slipped by, slow and lovely. Sometimes it seemed we had the whole river to ourselves. One morning I was heading up a creek in the canoe, looking for berries. All of a sudden, here comes a couple of men tearing along fast as they could. They called out and begged me to save their lives. They said they hadn't done nothing but was being chased for it—said there was men and dogs a-coming. I got them into the canoe and snuck back to the raft before anybody seen them.

One of these fellows was about 70 or more. And the other was about 30. We all had breakfast and laid off and talked. By and by the young fellow tells us he's the Duke of Bridgewater. He says he's been cheated out of his title and land. He lets on that Jim and me should wait on him and call him "My Lord." Then the old fellow says *he's* the Dauphin, cheated out of being the king of France. We should wait on him, too, and call him "Your Majesty."

I make up my mind pretty quick that these two were nothing but cheats and liars. But if I never learned nothing else from Pap, I learned the best way to get along with his kind of people is to let them have their own way.

They asked us a lot of questions. They wanted to know why we kept the raft hid and traveled at night. So I told them my folks was all dead and all I had left was my slave, Jim. But so many people thought he was a runaway slave and tried to take him away from me. So I kept him out of sight.

We stopped at a little one-horse town that was almost empty. Everybody was away at the camp meeting. The duke spotted an empty printing office with the door unlocked. So he said he'd fix up something to make it safe for Jim to travel in the daytime.

Me and the king lit out for the camp meeting. There under a shed was crowds of people and a preacher on a platform. He was shouting his words out with all his might. He'd shout, "Oh, come to the bench! Come, black with sin!" And the people would yell out, "Amen!" And they worked their way to the bench, shouting and crying.

Well, the first I knew the king got a-going, and you could hear him over everybody. He told the crowd he'd been a pirate, but now he was a changed man. He was going to the Indian Ocean to reform other pirates, even though it would take a long time because he had no money. In no time, people were singing out that he should pass his hat around, so he does. He got 87 dollars.

While we'd been at the meeting, the duke had printed up a poster saying Jim had run away from a plantation in New Orleans. The poster also said there was a 200-dollar reward for him. So whenever anyone asked questions about Jim we could say we'd caught him and was taking him back for the reward.

The king and duke figured they'd do scenes from Shakespeare in one of the towns. So for the next few days the raft was very lively, with sword fighting and speeches. The next town we landed at was called Bricksville. I was loafing around the main street that afternoon when somebody sings out, "Here comes old Boggs! He's in from the country for his little old monthly drunk."

Boggs comes tearing along on his horse. He was over 50 years old and had a very red face. He's whooping and yelling like an Indian, and he says he's going to kill old Colonel Sherburn. One of the men hanging around tells me, "He don't mean nothing. He's always a-carrying on like that when he's drunk."

Boggs rode up before the biggest store in town and starts calling Sherburn everything he could think of. By and by a proud-looking man about 55 steps out of the store. "I'm going to take this till one o'clock,

Boggs, and no longer," the man says.

Some men crowded around Boggs and tried to shut him up. About one o'clock it seemed like they'd finally got Boggs to quiet down. Then Sherburn steps out into the street with his gun. "Boggs!" he calls.

Boggs throws up his hands and says, "O Lord, don't shoot!" Bang! Bang! go the shots. Boggs falls to the ground. A few minutes later, he's dead.

Well, by and by somebody said Sherburn ought to be hung. In about a minute everybody was saying it. So away they went, mad and yelling, and snatching every clothesline they come across to do the hanging with. They swarmed up to Sherburn's house— children screaming and trying to get out of the way. You couldn't hear yourself think for the noise. They roll into Sherburn's yard and he steps out on his porch, perfectly calm, with a double-barrel gun. The racket stopped and the wave of people moved back.

Sherburn sort of laughs and says, "A mob like you is the most pitiful thing there is. You haven't got the bravery to hang a man unless you've got a *man* leading you. And you only brought half a man—Buck Harkness. Now leave and take your half-a-man with you." He cocked his gun and the crowd went tearing off every which way, with Buck Harkness after them.

That night the king and duke put on their show. But only 12 people come. So the next day they put out posters for a show called "The Royal Nonesuch," which says in big letters: "Ladies and children not admitted." That night the place was packed with men. The duke makes a speech and then the king comes out, naked and painted up like a rainbow. Never mind about the rest of his outfit. It was just as wild, but awful funny. And the things that old fool done would have made a cow laugh. But pretty quick the duke comes out and thanks everyone for coming. Twenty people sings out, "Is that *all?*"

The men was ready to come after the duke and king, but one man shouts out, "Hold on! We'll look like fools if we let on we've been cheated. Let's let the rest of the town be cheated, too. Then nobody can laugh at us." The men agreed, and the next day you couldn't hear nothing around that town but how fine that show was.

Next night the place was jammed again. The third night was another big crowd. And they weren't newcomers, but people who was at the first two shows. And they come with rotten eggs and cabbages and dead cats. As soon as everyone paid their money and got in the door, the duke told me to run for the raft, and we took off. Them cheats took in 465 dollars in those three nights. I never seen money hauled in like that before.

Next morning when I waked, Jim was sitting there with his head between his knees, moaning and sad. I knew what it was about. He was thinking about his wife and children, so far away. He often done that when he judged I was asleep.

This time I somehow got him talking about his wife and young ones. He was feeling bad about his daughter, 'Lizbeth. Jim told me that when she was one year old, she got scarlet fever. But she got well, and one day she was standing around and Jim says to her, "Shut the door."

She just kind of smiled at Jim, and it made him mad. He says it again, loud, but she just stands there. Finally he gives her a slap. Ten minutes later she's standing by the door and the wind blows it shut behind her, *ker-blam*! And she never moves! Jim busts out crying and takes her in his arms. "She's deaf and dumb," he says. "She is deaf and dumb, and I been a-treating her so!"

7 A Dirty Scheme

The king wanted to see what kind of money could be made in another little town down the river. So he sets out, with me paddling the canoe. Before we reach town we give a ride to a young country fellow who's on his way to New Orleans. This fellow thinks the king must be Harvey Wilks, come from England because his brother Peter just died. The fellow says Peter Wilks hadn't seen his brother Harvey, or William—who was deaf and dumb—since he was a child. But he left them a lot of money. Well, the king gets the fellow talking and finds out about Wilks's three nieces, his property and slaves, and everybody and everything in that blessed town.

When we leave the young fellow, the king has me go get the duke. I see what he was up to, but I never said nothing, of course. The king tells the duke all he knows. The king tells the duke to play William, the deaf and dumb brother, while he'll be Harvey.

The king pays for a boat ride into town, so he can arrive in style. About two dozen men flock out to meet it. The king asks where Peter Wilks lives. When they tell him Peter's dead, he says, "Oh, our poor brother—gone. Oh, it's too, too hard!" and busts out a-crying. Then he makes a lot of idiotic signs to the duke with his hands and *he* busts out a-crying. Well, the men gathered around and said all sorts of kind things to them. The king and duke carried on like it was their last day on earth. It was enough to make you ashamed of the human race.

Word spread around pretty quick. When we got to the Wilks's house it was packed with people, and the three nieces standing at the door. The king and duke put on another show of crying, and everybody joined in. Then the king asked about nearly everybody in town, as if he knew them all.

By and by the oldest niece, Mary Jane, read a letter written by Peter Wilks. The letter said he'd left the girls the house and 3,000 dollars in gold. He gave some property and another 3,000 to Harvey and William. And he told where the money was hid in the cellar.

The king said he and his so-called brother would go get the money and bring it upstairs. They found it and counted it—and it was 415 dollars short. The king says it's going to look suspicious when they take it upstairs and count it in front of everybody. So he and the duke they make up the money out of their own pockets.

Next morning, Joanna, the youngest niece, got to pumping me about what things were like in England. I didn't know much, and the ice got mighty thin.

After a while she said I was stretching the truth a lot.

Mary Jane heard that, and she lit into Joanna for being unkind to me. After all, I was a guest in the house and far away from my own folks. Then Susan, the middle niece, waltzes in and *she* gives Joanna another talking to. So Joanna apologizes and she done it beautiful.

I says to myself, *these* are the girls I'm letting that old snake rob of their money. I felt so low down and mean that I made my mind up. I'd get that money for them and hide it. Then when I was away down the river, I'd write a letter and tell Mary Jane where it's hid.

That night I went up to the bedroom they gave to the king. I began to paw around, when he and the duke both come in. I slipped behind a curtain where they hung the clothes. The duke tells the king he doesn't think they put the money in a good place. The king comes reaching in under the curtain two or three feet from where I was. I tried to think what I would say if they caught me. But he found the money bag pretty quick and they shoved it into a rip in the mattress.

I waited till they left, and then I took the bag. I got it downstairs when I heard someone coming down behind me. I run into the parlor and took a swift look around. The only place I see to hide the bag was the coffin. I tucked the bag in under the lid and hid behind the parlor door. The person coming was Mary Jane. She come up to the coffin, very soft, and kneeled down. Her back was to me, so I slid out and went back to my room.

The next afternoon was the funeral. I was in a sweat when the undertaker came up to close the coffin with his screwdriver. But he just slid the lid closed and went to work. I didn't know if the money was still in there or not.

Well, the king started talking about how he had to hurry back to England. He said he must sell the property right away. Two days after the funeral a couple of slave traders came along. So the king sold the two sons up to Memphis and their mother to New Orleans. I thought them poor nieces and them slaves would break their heart for sadness, they cried so.

Next morning the king and duke discovered the money was gone. They questioned me pretty close. I let on I'd seen the slaves come out of the king's room the day of the funeral. They blamed each other for that, then sassed me, and finally let me go.

8 The Scheme Comes Undone

A little later I was coming downstairs and I see Mary Jane in her room, crying. I asked her what was wrong and she says it was the slaves. She says, "They ain't *ever* going to see each other anymore!"

I says, "But they will—and I know it!"

I said it before I could think! She throws her arms around my neck and told me to say it *again*.

I was in a close place. I thought for a minute. Then I says I'll tell her if she'll promise to leave town till tonight. I knew that when I told her the truth, it would show on her face like big print. She promised she'd go stay with some folks. So I told her the slaves would be back soon because the sale weren't legal. Those uncles of hers weren't no uncles at all, but deadbeats and cheats.

I told her all about them. Her eyes were a-blazing. She wanted to have them tarred and feathered right away. But I told her we couldn't tell on them yet because we'd get someone she didn't know in big trouble. I wanted to get Jim out, and me too, before anyone put a hand on those two cheats.

I told her to put a candle in her window at eleven o'clock that night. I says, "If I don't turn up that means I'm gone, and safe. Then you come out and spread the news around, and get these deadbeats jailed." I told her if anyone needed proof about those two, they could talk to the folks of Bricksville.

Well, that afternoon, the steamboat come in and word spreads about how *another* couple of Wilks brothers just arrived. They brought a nice-looking old gentleman and a nice-looking younger one into town.

Well, people figured they'd better sit *both* sets of brothers down and find out which two were the real ones. They made the king tell his yarn, and they made the old gentleman tell his. Anybody but a lot of prejudiced chuckleheads would a-seen that the old gentleman was spinning truth and the other one lies.

Then the old gentleman says is there anybody here who laid Peter Wilks out before burying him. Someone says yes—him and another fellow. So the old man turns to the king and says, "Perhaps you can tell me what was tattooed on Peter's chest?"

The king turns a little white, and I figured he'd give it all up now. But he says it's a little blue arrow. Well, I never seen anything like the king for such out-and-out cheek.

Then the old gentleman says Peter had a "P—B— W" marked on his chest. But the men who laid Peter out says they didn't see nothing at all on his chest.

Well, everyone was in a state now. They grabbed the two brothers, and the king and duke and me. Then they marched us off to the graveyard to dig up the coffin. And if there weren't no tattoo on the body, they were going to hang us all.

I was kind of stunned, I was so scared. It was dark now, and a beautiful time to give the crowd a slip. But a big man took me by the wrist and I might as well try to give Goliath the slip.

We got to the grave, and they dug out the coffin and unscrewed the lid. Then someone sings out, "Gold!" Everyone pushes forward to get a look, and the man lets go of me. I lit out fast as I could.

As I run through town I see the candle in Mary Jane's window, and then I passed by. I got to the raft and says, "Come on out, Jim, and cut her loose. We're rid of them!"

Jim lit out of the wigwam, full of joy. In two seconds we went a-sliding down the river. It seemed so good to be free again and all by ourselves on the big river. But then I heard a boat, and here comes the king and the duke, as fast as they could. It was all I could do to keep from crying.

When they got aboard, the king got me by the collar. He says, "Trying to give us the slip, was ye!" He said he was going to drown me.

But the duke says: "Let him go, you old idiot! Would *you* have done any different?"

44

So the king let me go. They started blaming each other for losing out on all that money and property, as well as the 400 they made in Bricksville. But by and by the king got out his bottle and the duke tackled *his* and it weren't long before they were friendly again.

9 A Case of Mistaken Identity

After we'd traveled down the river a ways, the king and duke began to work the towns again. But luck weren't with them, and at last they were flat broke. Jim and me got uneasy. We figured they were so desperate they were going to rob somebody.

We stopped at a place called Pikesville. The king said he'd go into town to see if people had heard of "The Royal Nonesuch." After a while, me and the duke went after him. When we found him, he was pretty drunk. The king and duke starts to argue. The minute they were really going at it, I see my chance and run off as fast as I could.

I got to the raft and sung out, "Set her loose, Jim! We're all right now!" But there weren't no answer, and nobody come out of the wigwam. Jim was gone! I sat down and cried; I couldn't help it.

By and by I went out on the road, and run across a boy. He told me a runaway slave was just sold to a farmer named Silas Phelps, who lived two miles to the south. The fellow who sold him was an old man. He had a poster saying the slave had run away from New Orleans, and there was a reward for him. The old man said he couldn't wait around for the reward so he sold him to Phelps for 40 dollars.

I sat down to think. I couldn't see no way out of this trouble. After all this long journey, and all we'd done for those cheats, they'd gone and made Jim a slave again. For 40 dirty dollars!

Then it hit me that all this trouble was *my* doing. It was plain to see they'd been watching me from up there in heaven—watching while I helped a poor old woman's slave go free. And now I was getting a slap in the face for what I'd done.

My conscience kept grinding me, and at last I had an idea. I wrote a note to Miss Watson, telling her where Jim was. Right away I felt good, and washed clean of sin.

Then I got to thinking about traveling down the river. I see Jim before me all the time: in the day and in the nighttime, and we a-floating along, talking and laughing. I got to thinking about how he'd do everything he could think of for me, and how good he was.

I looked at that note, holding my breath. I says to myself, "All right, I'll go to hell"—and tore it up.

It was awful words, but they was said. I hid the raft at a woody island down the river, and sunk the canoe with rocks. Then I set out for Phelps's farm.

When I get there, a woman comes running out of the house, smiling all over. She says, "It's *you* at last! *Ain't* it?"

I says, "yes ma'am," before I thought.

She says to call her Aunt Sally. Then she says she wants to hear all about the whole family and how they're doing. I was about to give up and tell her the truth. But all of a sudden she grabbed me and pulled me behind the bed and told me to keep quiet.

An old gentleman comes in and Aunt Sally says, "Has he come yet?" And her husband says, no, he hasn't seen him. And then he goes on about how worried he is that the boy hasn't showed up yet. Then Aunt Sally pulls me up and says, "Well, here he is, Silas! It's *Tom Sawyer!*"

By jings, I almost fell through the floor! It was like being born again, I was so glad to find out who I was. And how they both did fire off questions about Aunt Polly and Sid and the rest of the family.

By and by I heard a steamboat coming up the river. I think, suppose Tom Sawyer's on that boat. So I told the folks I'd better go to town and get my baggage.

I started for town in their wagon and sure enough, I see Tom Sawyer coming along. When he sees me, his mouth falls open. He says, "I ain't never done you no harm. So what are you coming back to *haunt* me for?"

I says, "I ain't come back—I ain't been *gone*."

He says, "Honest now, you ain't a ghost? Weren't you ever murdered *at all?*"

I says, "No, I weren't ever murdered at all. I played it on them." Pretty quick he was satisfied I weren't dead. He wanted to hear all about what happened, but I said let it rest for now. I told him about the fix I was in, letting on I was Tom Sawyer.

He thought it over. Then he said I should take his trunk, put it in my wagon, and let on that it was mine. He said he'd come to the Phelps's about a half hour after me.

Then I tells him why I'm there—to steal Jim out of slavery. I says, "I know it's low down, but *I'm* low down. And I want you to keep quiet. Will you?"

His eye lit up and he says, "I'll help you!"

I couldn't believe it. Tom Sawyer a *slave* stealer.

"Oh, shucks," I said, "You're joking."

"I ain't joking."

"Well," I says, "joking or no joking, don't let on you know anything about a runaway slave."

I didn't want to spend too much time away, so I headed back to the Phelps's. About half an hour later, Tom shows up. He pretends he's Sid Sawyer, Tom's brother. Aunt Sally's pretty surprised. He tells her he wasn't really supposed to come, but begged and begged till Aunt Polly give in.

Me and Tom kept waiting for somebody to say something about the runaway slave. But nobody mentioned him until dinner. Then one of the children asks if he and Tom and me can go to the show tonight. Uncle Silas says there isn't going to be any show. The runaway slave told him all about that show, and he spread the word. So they should have run those two cheats out of town by now.

So there it was! I figured I'd better warn the king and duke or they'd get in trouble, sure. After Tom and me went up to bed, we snuck down the lightning rod and headed for town.

On the way, Tom told me how Pap disappeared after everybody thought I'd been killed. And he said there'd been such a stir when Jim run away. I was telling him as much about the raft voyage as I had time to. As we struck into town here comes a raging rush of people with torches. There was an awful whooping and yelling, and we jumped to one side to let them go by.

They had the king and the duke riding on a rail, and they was covered all over with tar and feathers. They didn't look like nothing in the world that was human. Well, it made me sick to see such a sight. It seemed like I couldn't feel any hardness against those two ever again. Human beings *can* be awful cruel to one another.

10 Tom's Plan

We seen a slave carrying food down to a hut, so Tom figures they've got Jim in there. Next we're talking about a plan to get him out. My plan was to steal the key from Uncle Silas and take Jim down the river on the raft. Then Tom told me *his* plan, and it was worth 15 of mine for style.

Well, one thing was dead sure, and that was Tom Sawyer was really going to help steal Jim out of slavery. Here was a boy that was respectable, and he was about to shame himself and his family. I tried to tell him he ought to quit this thing right now. But he shut me up, and I knew it weren't no use to say any more.

The slave who fed Jim was a fellow called Nat. He had his hair tied up in bunches to keep witches away. He says come along and see what's in the hut. I didn't want to, but Tom said yes. Sure enough, as soon as Jim sees us, he sings out. "Why *Huck*! And good land! Ain't that Mister Tom?"

Nat says, "why, gracious sakes! Do he know you gentlemen?"

But Tom tells him that nobody said anything at all. He says, "What's the matter with you, anyway?

What made you think somebody sung out?" Nat says it must have been the witches, and please don't tell nobody about it. Tom said we wouldn't tell.

Tom figured we'd need a sheet, to make an escape ladder for Jim. And we'd need a shirt, too, that Jim could write a journal on. I said Jim couldn't write, but Tom said he could make marks on it. That's the way they done it in all the books. So I borrowed a sheet and a white shirt off the clothesline.

We figured we had to free Jim before Uncle Silas found out he hadn't really escaped from a plantation in New Orleans. That very night we set out to dig a tunnel under the hut. Tom said we had to dig with knives, because prisoners never had anything modern such as shovels. We tried it, but all we got was blisters. So Tom says let's use picks and pretend they're knives. After that, the work went pretty quick.

By the next night, the tunnel was done, and we were inside the hut. Jim was so glad to see us he most cried. He was for having us cut the chain off his leg and free him right away. But Tom sat down and told him all our plans, and said not to be afraid. We'd set him free by and by. He told Jim to be on the lookout, because Nat would be bringing him a rope ladder made in a pie.

Next morning, when Nat came to feed Jim, Tom told him the witches kept coming around Jim's hut because they was hungry. What they needed was a witch pie, and Tom would make him one. That pleased Nat no end.

Well, pretty quick Aunt Sally misses the things we took. So we'd put something back where it was and then steal it again. By and by, she didn't know how many sheets or whatever she had, or where they were.

But that pie was a job. We fixed it up and cooked it down in the woods. We didn't want nothing but a crust. But when we cooked the thing, it kept caving in, because there weren't nothing to prop it up. At last we thought of the right way, which was to cook the ladder inside the pie. We tore up the sheet in little strings and twisted them together and made a lovely rope ladder. Then we lined a pan with dough, stuck the ladder in, and made a dough roof. Nat brought it to the hut the next day, thinking it was a witch pie.

Tom wanted to bring a lot of rats and snakes and spiders into Jim's hut, so that Jim could tame them. Jim didn't like that idea much. But Tom said that all the prisoners in books made pets out of such animals, and he must do it, too.

We bought a wire trap and caught about 15 rats down in the cellar. We put the trap in a safe place under Aunt Sally's bed. But while we was gone for spiders one of Aunt Sally's boys found it. He opened the door to see if the rats would come out, and they did. When we come back Aunt Sally was on top of the bed raising Cain, and the rats were making things lively for her. We got a whipping for that, though Aunt Sally's whippings didn't amount to anything. It took us two hours to catch another batch.

By and by we got everything into Jim's hut. Between the rats and spiders and snakes, there weren't hardly no room for him. Jim said if he got free he wouldn't ever be a prisoner again, not even for pay.

11 The Escape

Uncle Silas had written a couple of times to the plantation in New Orleans. He told them they could come get their slave. But of course he hadn't got an answer because there weren't any such plantation. So he figured he'd advertise Jim in the St. Louis and New Orleans papers. That meant we hadn't time to lose.

Tom says it's time to write letters warning people about Jim's escape. I didn't like the idea, but Tom said that's the way it had to be done. He writes this letter saying a gang of cutthroats is coming the next night to free the slave. He signs it, "Unknown Friend."

Next day we went to look at the raft, and we found her all right. When we got home, everyone was in such a sweat and worry they didn't know which end they was standing on. They wouldn't tell us what the trouble was, but we knew.

They sent us to bed right after supper. On the way, we sneaked us a good lunch from the cellar and took it up to our room. We went to bed and woke up about half past eleven. We was starting out with the lunch when Tom says there ain't no butter. He said I should slide down to the cellar and get it.

So out he went to Jim's hut and I went back for the butter.

I got a hunk of butter and corn pone, but here comes Aunt Sally. So I clapped the stuff under my hat. She says I've been up to something and marches me into the sitting room. My, but there was a crowd there! Fifteen farmers, and every one of them had a gun. They're talking about the gang of cutthroats that's supposed to be coming. I was in a sweat to get away and tell Tom we'd overdone this thing and had to clear out right away. But Aunt Sally's asking me questions about what I'm doing up this time of night. I couldn't answer her straight, I was so scared.

The room got hotter and hotter, and a streak of butter comes a-trickling down my forehead. Aunt Sally turns white as a sheet. She says, "Land's sake! He's got the brain fever, and his brains are oozing out!" She snatches off my hat and out comes the bread and butter. She grabbed me and hugged me, and says, "Why didn't you *tell* me that was all you'd been down to the cellar for. I wouldn't a-cared. Now clear out to bed, and don't let me see you till morning!"

I got out of the house and into the hut just as the men was coming outside. We got into the tunnel, swift but quiet—Jim first, me next, and Tom last. We crawled through and out the hole and up to the fence. Me and Jim got over it, but Tom's pants caught on a

splinter. The splinter snapped and somebody sings
out: "Who's that? Answer, or I'll shoot!" We ran. There
was a rush, and a *bang, bang, bang!* The bullets
whizzed around us! We heard them sing out: "They've
gone for the river! Turn loose the dogs!"

The dogs come, but when they see it weren't
nobody but us, they just said howdy and went tearing
along. We struck through the brush to the canoe.
Then we paddled for dear life out to the middle of
the river. But soon we was so far away we couldn't
hardly hear all the barking and yelling. When we got
to the island where the raft was hid, we was all glad

as we could be. But Tom was gladdest of all because he had a bullet in his leg.

He was all for heading out, but me and Jim said we'd got to go for a doctor. Tom raised a fuss, and give us a piece of his mind. But we wouldn't budge. I left for town. Jim was going to stay with Tom. He said he'd hide in the woods when the doctor came.

12 Surprises All Around

The doctor was a very nice old man. I told him me and my brother was camping over at the island when his gun went off and shot him in the leg. I asked if he could go out to the island and fix his leg and not tell anybody about it. We wanted to surprise the folks. He asked me some questions, but finally he come along.

When we got to the canoe, he said it looked too small for both of us. So I told him how to find Tom and he set out alone. I figured after a while I'd shove along for the island, too. I crept into a lumber pile to get some sleep. Next time I waked up, the sun was away up over my head! I thought I'd better get to the island right off. So away I shoved, and turned the corner, and nearly rammed my head into Uncle Silas's stomach! He says, "Why, Tom! Where have you been all this time? Your aunt's been mighty uneasy."

I said we'd been out hunting the slave who run away. I told him "Sid" was waiting at the post office, in case there was any news. We went to the post office, but of course "Sid" didn't show up, so we went on home.

Aunt Sally was so glad to see me she laughed and cried both. She give me one of them whippings that didn't amount to anything. And she said she'd give "Sid" the same when he came home.

The house was full of farmers and farmers' wives. They went on about the escaped slave and all the strange things left in the hut. And Aunt Sally said it must have been the work of spirits, because the dogs never even got on the track of 'em.

When it got dark and Tom still hadn't showed up, Aunt Sally was a good deal uneasy. When I went up to bed, she came up with me. She talked about what a fine boy Sid was. She kept asking if I figured he could have gotten lost or hurt, and her tears dripped down silent. When she was going away she said, "The door ain't going to be locked, Tom. But you'll be good, won't you?"

Well, I *wanted* to go bad enough to see about Tom. But after she said that, I couldn't go, not for anything.

Next morning Uncle Silas says he has a letter from Aunt Sally's sister, who is Tom's Aunt Polly. But before Sally could open the letter, she dropped it and run. A lot of people was coming up to the house. They had Tom Sawyer on a mattress. They had Jim, too, with his hands tied behind his back. I hid the letter and rushed out.

Aunt Sally flung herself at Tom, crying. Tom muttered something or other, which showed he weren't in his right mind. Aunt Sally says, "He's alive!" and flew for the house to get the bed ready. I followed the men to see what they'd do to Jim.

Some of the men wanted to hang Jim. But the others said don't do it, because his owner would show up and make them pay for him. So they cussed Jim, and hit him, and chained him up again.

Then the doctor comes out and says, "Don't be too rough on him, because he ain't bad. When I got out on the island and found the boy, I see I couldn't cut the bullet out without some help. And the boy got worse and worse and went out of his head. He wouldn't let me come near him. So I says out loud, 'I got to have *help* somehow.' The minute I says it, out crawls this slave from somewhere and says he'll help. And he done it very well."

After that the men softened up, and I was mighty thankful to that old doctor.

Next morning Tom was better, so I slipped into his room. I thought if he was awake, we could make up some kind of story to tell the family. But then Aunt Sally comes in, too, and I'm stuck. By and by Tom opens his eyes very natural and says, "Why, I'm at *home*! Where's the raft? and Jim?"

"They're all right," I says.

He says, "Good! Did you tell Aunty about how we set the slave free?"

Aunt Sally thinks he's out of his head again, but he tells her all about it. He tells her about how we had to steal the sheet and shirt, and about the rats and spiders and everything else.

Aunt Sally says she's never heard the likes of such a story. She said she'd give us both a whipping when Tom got well. And if she caught us meddling with the slave again . . .

Tom says "What do you mean? Didn't he get away?"

Aunt Sally says no, they've got him safe and sound, chained up in the hut.

Well, Tom sits right up, with his eyes hot. He says, "They ain't got no *right* to shut him up! He's free! Old

Miss Watson, who owned him, died two months ago. And she was so ashamed she was ever going to sell him down the river, she set him free in her will."

Aunt Sally says, "Well, why on earth did *you* want to set him free for, if he was already free?"

Tom says, "Why, I wanted the *adventure* of it! And I'd a-waded neck-deep in blood to—goodness sakes! Aunt Polly's here!"

And there she was, standing at the door! Aunt Sally jumped for her, and most hugged the head off her. And of course Aunt Polly turns to Tom and calls him Tom, *not* Sid. And lets Aunt Sally know I'm Huck Finn, and not Tom at all. So Tom and I had to tell them all about *that*.

Then Aunt Polly says, "Tom's right about Jim being free. Until this minute, I couldn't understand how somebody with Tom Sawyer's bringing-up could help free a slave."

We had Jim out of chains in no time and Tom give him 40 dollars for being such a patient prisoner. Jim was most pleased to death. Then Tom says, "Let's all three of us take off for Indian territory and go for some adventures." But I figured I was too broke, because Pap's probably been back and got all my money.

Jim says, "He ain't a-coming back no more."

He wouldn't tell me why, but I kept at him. At last he says, "Remember when we went on that house

66

that was floating down the river? And there was a dead man lying there? That was your Pap."

Tom's most well now, and he wears his bullet around his neck. And so there ain't nothing more to write about, and I am rotten glad of it. If I knew what a trouble it was to make a book I wouldn't a-tackled it, and I ain't going to no more. I figure I got to light out for the Territory ahead of the others. Aunt Sally's going to adopt me and civilize me and I can't stand it. I been there before.

The End
Yours Truly, Huck Finn